Congressional
Research Service
Informing the legislative debate since 1914 _____

Defense Acquisition Reform: Background, Analysis, and Issues for Congress

Moshe Schwartz
Specialist in Defense Acquisition

May 23, 2014

Congressional Research Service

7-5700

www.crs.gov

R43566

Summary

The Department of Defense (DOD) relies extensively on contractors to equip and support the U.S. military in peacetime and during military operations, obligating more than $300 billion on contracts in FY2013.

Congress and the executive branch have long been frustrated with waste, mismanagement, and fraud in defense acquisitions and have spent significant resources attempting to reform and improve the process. These frustrations have led to numerous efforts to improve defense acquisitions. Since the end of World War II, every Administration and virtually every Secretary of Defense has embarked on an acquisition reform effort. Yet despite these efforts, cost overruns, schedule delays, and performance shortfalls in acquisition programs persist.

A number of analysts have argued that the successive waves of acquisition reform have yielded only limited results due in large part to poor workforce management. Most reports have concluded that the key to good acquisitions is having a sufficiently sized and talented acquisition workforce and giving them the resources, incentives, and authority to do their job. Yet most of the reform efforts of the past decades have not sought to fundamentally and systematically address these workforce-related issues.

Significant changes to the national security and industrial landscape in recent years, including consolidation of the defense industrial base and the increasing complexity of weapon systems, have led many analysts to call for a renewed effort to improve the acquisition process.

Historically, eras of budgetary restraint have been associated with the pursuit and implementation of acquisition reform. Against the current backdrop of the Budget Control Act of 2011 and declines in defense spending, the stage may be set for a renewed effort to significantly improve defense acquisitions. Other factors contributing to a sense among analysts that the time may be ripe for reform include recent experiences in Iraq and Afghanistan and the increasing availability of data to drive decisions.

In recent years, DOD has taken a number of steps to improve the process by which it buys goods and services, including

- rewriting the regulatory structure that governs defense acquisitions;

- launching the *Better Buying Power* and *Better Buying Power II* initiatives aimed at improving the productivity of the acquisition system and the industrial base;

- improving the use of data to support decision making; and

- establishing a team to develop a legislative proposal aimed at simplifying the laws and regulations governing defense acquisitions.

Many analysts believe that what DOD can do on its own to improve acquisitions can only go so far—that significant, effective, and lasting acquisition reform will occur only with the active participation of Congress. Congress has been critical to advancing acquisition reform; such efforts as establishing the Federal Acquisition Regulation, creating Defense Acquisition University, streamlining acquisition regulations, and enacting the Goldwater-Nichols Act were the result of congressional action.

Oversight issues for Congress include the extent to which the Weapon System Acquisition Reform Act of 2009 (P.L. 111-23) and the various DOD initiatives are having a positive effect on acquisitions, whether current reform efforts are sufficient to address concerns related to the acquisition workforce, and what additional steps, if any, Congress can take to further the effort to improve defense acquisitions.

Contents

Figures

Appendixes

Contacts

Introduction

The Department of Defense (DOD) relies extensively on contractors to equip and support the U.S. military in peacetime and during military operations. Contractors design, develop, and build advanced weapon and business systems, construct military bases around the world, and provide services such as intelligence analysis, logistics, and base support. For as long as the U.S. military has relied on contractors, DOD and Congress have sought to improve the cost, schedule, and performance of the goods and services being acquired. Pursuit of this goal has often taken the form of seeking to identify and implement effective reforms of the acquisition process.

This report provides background information and identifies issues for Congress when contemplating acquisition reform. Related CRS products include *Defense Acquisitions: What Can We Learn From Past Reform Efforts?*, a multi-part video series that reflects on past defense acquisition reform efforts. See **Appendix C** for the syllabus accompanying the course on acquisition reform. To view the series, see

- CRS Report WVB00020, Defense Acquisitions: What Can We Learn From Past Reform Efforts?, by Moshe Schwartz

- CRS Report WVB00022, Defense Acquisitions: The Foundation of Modern Acquisition Reform (1970-1986): The Fitzhugh and Packard Reports, by Moshe Schwartz

- CRS Report WVB00024, Defense Acquisitions: The 1990s: The Perry Report, Section 800 Panel, and More, by Moshe Schwartz

Related CRS reports include CRS Report RL34026, *Defense Acquisitions: How DOD Acquires Weapon Systems and Recent Efforts to Reform the Process*, by Moshe Schwartz; CRS Report R41293, *The Nunn-McCurdy Act: Background, Analysis, and Issues for Congress*; and CRS Report R43074, *Department of Defense's Use of Contractors to Support Military Operations: Background, Analysis, and Issues for Congress.*

Background

In FY2013, DOD obligated $310 billion on federal contracts—more than half (51%) of total DOD direct obligations and more than the contract obligations of all other federal government agencies combined (**Figure 1**).[1] DOD contract obligations were equivalent to approximately 9% of the entire U.S. budget.[2]

---

[1] Calculations are based on total contract obligations data as recorded in the Federal Procurement Data System—Next Generation, February 2014. FPDS-NG does not include data from judicial branch agencies, the legislative branch, certain DOD components, or select executive branch agencies, such as the Central Intelligence Agency and National Security Agency. See also United States Department of the Treasury, "Joint Statement of Secretary Lew and OMB Director Burwell on Budget Results for Fiscal Year 2013 ," press release, October 30, 2013, http://www.treasury.gov/press-center/press-releases/Pages/jl2197.aspx.

[2] For purposes of this report, total obligations are defined as total direct obligations. Deflators for converting into constant dollars derived from Office of the Under Secretary of Defense (Comptroller), *National Defense Budget Estimates for FY 3013*, Department of Defense, "Department of Defense Deflators – TOA by Category 'Total Non-(continued...)

Figure 1. Contract Obligations, by Agency
FY2013

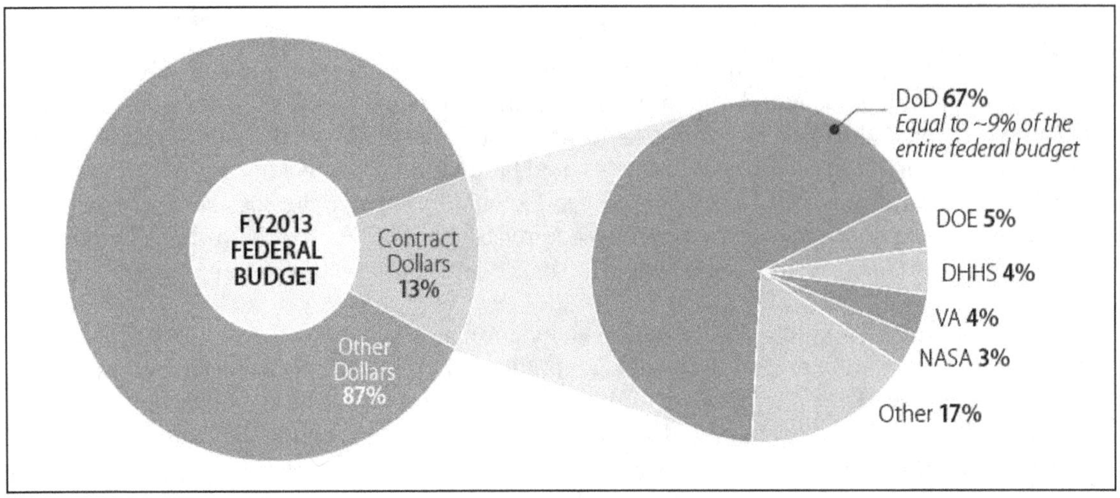

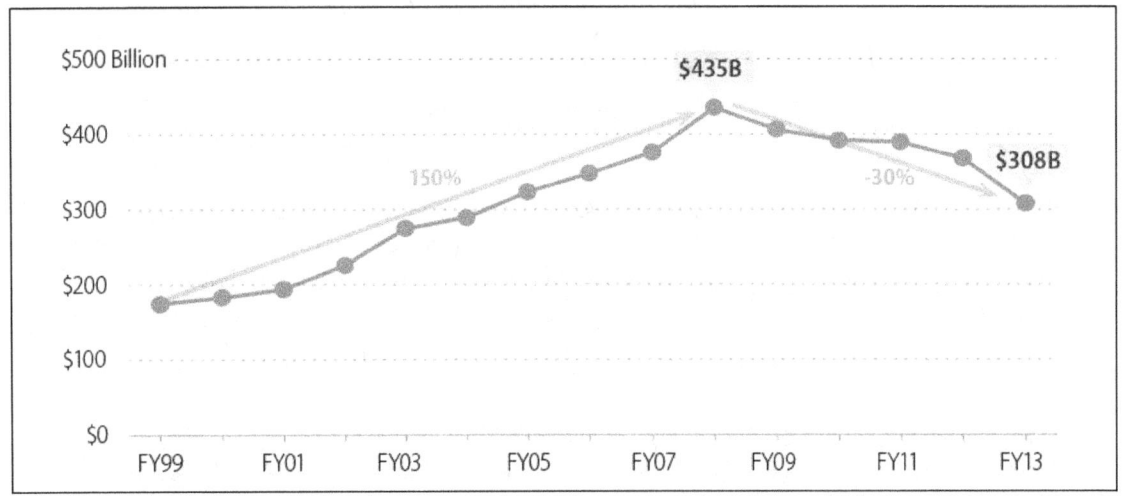

DoD **67%**
Equal to ~9% of the entire federal budget

DOE **5%**

DHHS **4%**

VA **4%**

NASA **3%**

Other **17%**

FY2013 FEDERAL BUDGET

Contract Dollars **13%**

Other Dollars **87%**

Source: Federal Procurement Data System-Next Generation, February, 2014. Figure by CRS Graphics.

Note: DOE – Department of Energy; DHHS – Department of Health and Human Services; VA – Department of Veterans Affairs; NASA - National Aeronautics and Space Administration.

From FY1999 through FY2013, adjusted for inflation (FY2013 dollars), DOD contract obligations increased from $175 billion to $308 billion (see **Figure 2**). Over the first part of this period—FY1999 through FY2008—contract obligations increased 150%, from $175 billion to $435 billion. This trend reversed itself in FY2008: from FY2008 through FY2013, contract obligations decreased by 30%, dropping from $435 billion to $308 billion.

Figure 2. DOD Contract Obligations (FY2013 dollars)
FY1999-FY2013 (in billions)

Source: CRS analysis of data from the Federal Procurement Data System—Next Generation, February 2014.

(...continued)

Pay,'" Table 5-5, pp. 59-60, March, 2012.

In FY2013, the acquisition of services represented 52% of total DOD contract obligations (including research and development) compared to 48% for goods (see **Figure 3**). Despite more than half of contract obligations being dedicated to the acquisition of services over the last two decades, past reform efforts have tended to focus on the acquisition of goods—with particular attention paid to weapon systems.

Figure 3. Percentage of Contract Obligations, by Category

FY1998-FY2013

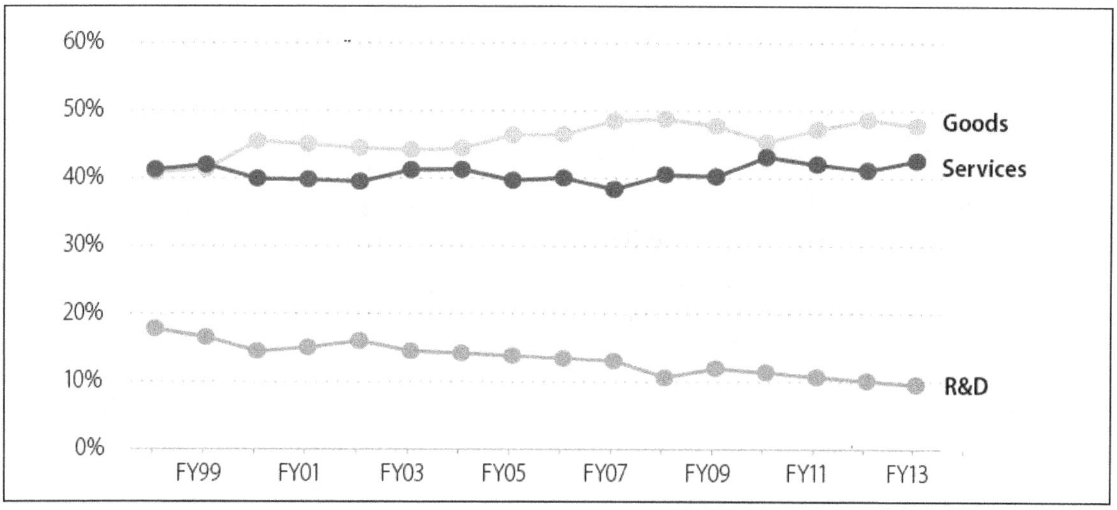

Source: CRS Analysis of data from the Federal Procurement Data System, February 2014.

Note: R&D is broken out as a separate category to highlight the trend in R&D obligations.

Prior Efforts to Improve Acquisitions

Congress and the executive branch have long been frustrated with waste, mismanagement, and fraud in defense acquisitions and have spent significant resources seeking to reform and improve the process. Efforts to address wasteful spending, cost overruns, schedule slips, and performance shortfalls have continued unabated, with more than 150 major studies on acquisition reform since the end of World War II. Every Administration and virtually every Secretary of Defense has embarked on an acquisition reform effort.[3]

In the early 1980s a number of major weapon system programs experienced dramatic cost overruns—overruns that increased the defense budget by billions of dollars but resulted in the production of the same number of, or in some cases fewer, weapons than originally planned. In 1985, President Ronald Reagan established the *President's Blue Ribbon Commission on Defense Management*, chaired by former Deputy Secretary of Defense David Packard, which issued a final report (known as the Packard Commission Report) that contained far-reaching recommendations "intended to assist the Executive and Legislative Branches as well as industry in implementing a broad range of needed reforms." In 1994, then Secretary of Defense William

---

[3] Robert F. Hale, *Promoting Efficiency in the Department of Defense: Keep Trying, Be Realistic,* Center for Strategic and Budgetary Assessments, January 2002, p. 7.

Perry released a blueprint for another round of reform efforts in the report *Acquisition Reform: A Mandate for Change.*[4]

Congress has also been active in pursuing reform, legislating changes through the annual National Defense Authorization Acts and through stand-alone legislation, such as the Defense Acquisition Workforce Improvement Act of 1990,[5] Federal Acquisition Streamlining Act of 1994,[6] Clinger-Cohen Act of 1996,[7] and Weapon System Acquisition Reform Act of 2009.[8] A number of these efforts were aimed at implementing recommendations of the Packard and Perry reports.

The various reform efforts have dramatically altered the process by which DOD procures goods and services. Major changes include

- creating the Federal Acquisition Regulation (FAR) to develop uniform acquisition regulations across DOD and the federal government;

- establishing Defense Acquisition University to train and improve the performance of the acquisition workforce;

- instituting a streamlined management chain (Program Manager, Program Executive Office, Service Acquisition Executive, Under Secretary of Defense) to foster accountability and authority;

- implementing a milestone decision process to improve oversight;

- requiring independent cost estimates to improve budget forecasting;[9]

- establishing a joint requirements board to improve requirements development and eliminate duplicative programs;

- moving away from the use of customized military standards and specifications to increased use of commercial technologies; and

- using multi-year procurements (with congressional approval) to lower costs.

Cost, Schedule, and Performance Problems Persist

Acquisition programs initiated since the 1970s have continued to experience significant cost increases and other problems.[10] As one RAND report stated, "despite the many acquisition

---

[4] Honorable William J. Perry, *Acquisition Reform: A Mandate for Change*, Department of Defense, February 9, 1994.

[5] P.L. 101-510.

[6] P.L. 103-355.

[7] P.L. 104-106.

[8] P.L. 111-23.

[9] The Cost Analysis and Improvement Group was established within the Office of the Secretary of Defense in 1972 to develop these independent cost estimates. Today, independent cost estimates are generated by the Office of the Director of Cost Assessment and Program Evaluation, which supplanted the Cost Analysis and Improvement Group.

[10] See David S. Christensen, Ph.D., Capt. David A. Searle, USAF, and Dr. Caisse Vickery, "The Impact of the Packard Commission's Recommendations on Reducing Cost Overruns on Defense Acquisition Contracts," *Acquisition Review Quarterly*, Summer 1999, p. 251; Deloitte Consulting LLP, *Can We Afford Our Own Future? Why A&D Programs are Late and Over-budget—and What Can Be Done to Fix the Problem*, 2008; U.S. Congress, Senate Committee on Homeland Security and Governmental Affairs, Subcommittee on Federal Financial Management, Government Information, Federal Services, and International Security, Comments of Michael J. Sullivan, Government
(continued...)

---

reforms and other DoD management initiatives over the years, the development cost growth of military systems has not been reduced."[11] Consider the following:

- Since 1993, development contracts have experienced a median of 32% cost growth (not adjusted for inflation).[12]

- Since 1997, 31% of all Major Defense Acquisition Programs (MDAP) have had cost growth of at least 15%.[13]

- During the period 1990-2010, the Army terminated 22 Major Defense Acquisition Programs; every year between 1996 and 2010, the Army spent more than $1 billion on programs that were ultimately cancelled.[14]

- Procurement costs for the aircraft carrier CVN-78 have grown more than 20% since the submission of the FY2008 budget, and 4% since the submission of the FY2013 budget, prompting the Navy to program more than $1.3 billion in additional procurement funding for the ship in FY2014 and FY2015.[15]

Can Acquisition Reform Succeed?

Given the results of past efforts, some analysts have argued that acquisition reform is a fruitless effort and that the fundamental problems with DOD acquisitions lie not in policy but in execution and expectations. In an article entitled *Let's Skip Acquisition Reform This Time*, MIT professor Harvey Sapolsky wrote

> The limited number of available reforms have all been recycled. You can centralize or decentralize. You can create a specialist acquisition corps or you can outsource their tasks. You can fly before you buy or buy before you fly. Another blue-ribbon study, more legislation, and a new slogan will not make it happen.[16]

A number of analysts have also argued that far from improving the system, many past reform efforts have made the process less efficient and effective.[17] A recent report on Army acquisitions

---

(...continued)

Accountability Office, *Tools to Prevent Defense Department Cost Overruns*, 112th Cong., 1st sess., March 29, 2011.

[11] See Obaid Yousossi, Mark V. Arena, and Robert S. Leonard, et al., *Is Weapon System Cost Growth Increasing?*, RAND, Santa Monica, CA, 2007, p. xx.

[12] Office of the Under Secretary of Defense Acquisition, Technology and Logistics, *Performance of the Defense Acquisition System*, 2013 Annual Report, June 28, 2013, p. 28.

[13] Based on percentage of programs experiencing Nunn-McCurdy breach. Office of the Under Secretary of Defense Acquisition, Technology and Logistics, *Performance of the Defense Acquisition System*, 2013 Annual Report, June 28, 2013, p. 20.

[14] U.S. Army, *Army Strong: Equipped, Trained and Ready*, Final Report of the 2010 Army Acquisition Review, January 11, 2011, p. ix.

[15] CRS Report RS20643, *Navy Ford (CVN-78) Class Aircraft Carrier Program: Background and Issues for Congress*, by Ronald O'Rourke, p. 9.

[16] Harvey Sapolsky, "Let's Skip Acquisition Reform This Time," *DefenseNews*, February 9, 2009, p. 29.

[17] U.S. Institute for Peace, *The QDR in Perspective: Meeting America's National Security Needs in the 21st Century*, Final Report of the Quadrennial Defense Review Independent Panel, July 28, 2010, p. 83; Department of Defense, *Defense Acquisition Performance Assessment Report*, January 2006, p. 6; Business Executives for National Security, *Getting to Best: Reforming the Defense Acquisition Enterprise*, A Business Imperative for Change from the Task Force on Defense Acquisition Law and Oversight, July, 2009, p. iii.

argued "in an attempt to not repeat past failures, additional staff, processes, steps, and tasks have been imposed. While well intended, collectively these modifications are counterproductive."[18] One observer noted, "If someone were asked to devise a contracting system for the federal government, it is inconceivable that one reasonable person or a committee of reasonable people could come up with our current system."[19]

Some analysts point out that some past reform efforts have had modest success, generating savings in certain areas and keeping pace with a changing world. For example, most analysts view the original consolidation of disparate acquisition rules into a single, uniform Federal Acquisition Regulation as an improvement to the system. More recently, Congress has embarked on select acquisition reform efforts through legislation that some (but not all) analysts believe have contributed to improving defense acquisitions, including the *Weapon Systems Reform Act of 2009* and efforts to improve operational contract support. Many of these analysts believe that learning from past reform efforts—understanding what worked, what did not work, and why—is critical to successful acquisition reform.[20]

The Weapon Systems Acquisition Reform Act

In developing the *Weapon Systems Acquisition Reform Act of 2009*, Congress considered reports by government and other analysts that focused on the early stages of weapon system development, prior congressional hearings and investigations, and extensive consultations with DOD, industry, and outside experts. The act did not seek to rectify all of the problems related to the acquisition process. Rather, it focused primarily on improving the early stages of weapon system development. Key provisions in the act included

- appointment of a Director of Cost Assessment and Program Evaluation (CAPE);

- appointment of a Director of Developmental Test and Evaluation;

- appointment of a Director of Systems Engineering;

- a requirement that the Director of Defense Research and Engineering periodically assess technological maturity of MDAPs and annually report finding to Congress; and

- a requirement that combatant commanders have more influence in the requirements generation process.

The full effect of the Weapon System Acquisition Reform Act may not be quantifiable until the next generation of weapon systems are in production. However, a number of analysts believe that the act is already having a positive effect.[21] Senior officials within the Offices of the CAPE, Developmental Test and Evaluation, and Systems Engineering believe that their offices were

---

[18] U.S. Army, *Army Strong: Equipped, Trained and Ready*, Final Report of the 2010 Army Acquisition Review, January 11, 2011, p. iv

[19] J. Ronald Fox, *Defense Acquisition Reform 1960-2009: An Elusive Goal* (Center of Military History, 2011).

[20] See Robert F. Hale, *Promoting Efficiency in the Department of Defense: Keep Trying, Be Realistic*, Center for Strategic and Budgetary Assessments, January2002, p. 7.

[21] U.S. Government Accountability Office, *Defense Acquisition Reform: Reform Act is Helping DOD Acquisition Programs Reduce Risk, but Implementation Challenges Remain*, GAO-13-103, December 14, 2012.

empowered to positively impact weapon system acquisitions.[22] These offices have been given access to senior leaders within the department, opportunities to provide input at key points in the acquisition system, and resources to carry out their responsibilities. For example, the CAPE has contributed to a better understanding of potential costs for a number of major programs, such as the F-35 Joint Strike Fighter program.[23] The act's focus on the early stage of the acquisition process and on using data to inform decisions complements and reinforces a number of the current internal DOD initiatives to improve acquisitions. However, some analysts have raised concerns that the offices created or empowered by the act are not sufficiently funded or manned to accomplish their mission.[24]

Operational Contract Support

In recent years, DOD has significantly improved its use of operational contract support.[25] Many analysts and senior DOD officials have stated that without the efforts of Congress, DOD would not have been as successful at improving operational contract support.[26] Congressional efforts have included establishing the Special Inspector General for Iraq Reconstruction, the Special Inspector General for Afghanistan Reconstruction, and the Commission on Wartime Contracting in Iraq and Afghanistan. Congress has also held numerous hearings, published reports, and maintained focus on the issue.

These efforts have combined to elevate within DOD the recognition of the importance of the use of contractors, and resulted in the development of a body of work that informed DOD and Congress. Other examples of congressional action cited as having contributed to improving operational contract support including the following:

- legislation that led to establishment of the office of the Deputy Assistant Secretary of Defense (Program Support);

- legislation establishing general/flag officer billets for acquisition;

- legislation creating the Defense Acquisition Workforce Development Fund;

- legislation requiring the increased integration of contractor scenarios into training and education; and

- oversight hearings that raised awareness of contractor abuses and led to the creation of Task Force 2010.[27]

---

[22] Based on meetings these senior officials had with CRS in early 2011.

[23] Based on discussions with senior officials from the Joint Staff, J-8 (Force Structure, Resources, and Assessment Directorate) and Joint Operations Support (Acquisition, Technology & Logistics), December 2011.

[24] U.S. Congress, Senate Committee on Armed Services, *Reform of the Defense Acquisition System*, Written Testimony of Jonathan Etherton, 113th Cong., 2nd sess., April 30, 2014.

[25] Operational contract support is the term used in DOD doctrine to describe the use of contractors to support military operations. For a full discussion, see CRS Report R43074, *Department of Defense's Use of Contractors to Support Military Operations: Background, Analysis, and Issues for Congress*, by Moshe Schwartz.

[26] Ibid.

[27] Task Force 2010 was established in 2010 to help DOD commanders and acquisition personnel better understand with whom they are doing business, to conduct investigations to gain visibility into the flow of money at the subcontractor level, and to promote best contracting practices. For a detailed discussion of reform in operational contract support, see CRS Report R43074, *Department of Defense's Use of Contractors to Support Military Operations: Background, Analysis, and Issues for Congress*, by Moshe Schwartz.

The Changing Landscape of Defense Acquisitions

Much of the organization of the defense acquisition system was developed during the early years of the Cold War. In recent years, the defense acquisition landscape has changed significantly, and a number of analysts believe that the acquisition system is not sufficiently responsive to an ever-changing world.[28] A 2009 study by the Defense Science Board argued that current DOD acquisition practices are inadequate in a changing industrial landscape.[29] Significant changes shaping the acquisition environment often cited by analysts include the following:

- *The defense industrial base has consolidated significantly over the last 25 years.* According to a study by the Defense Science Board, over the last 25 years, the number of major defense contractors decreased from 50 to 6.[30] Such consolidation, which was partly due to the reduction in defense procurement following the end of the Cold War, can have benefits but can also hurt competition and innovation.

- *DOD is becoming a less influential buyer.* Fewer U.S. industries are dominated by defense spending.[31] For example, in 1965, DOD accounted for over 75% of all U.S. semiconductor purchases. By 1990, government-wide purchases represented less than 10% of the market. By 2012, government represented less than 2% of the semi-conductor market.[32]

  As DOD becomes a less important customer, an increasing number of companies are diversifying their revenue streams. In 2012, the top 100 defense companies received 28% of their revenue from defense contracts, down from 38% of revenue in 2007.[33] Other companies are choosing not to compete for defense contracts because of extensive and ever-changing regulations, increased costs, auditing requirements, and instability of funding caused by sequestration, continuing resolutions, and lapses in appropriations.

- *Weapon and business systems are more complex and sophisticated.* Some analysts believe that the acquisition system is not nimble enough for acquisition programs that rely heavily on rapidly changing technologies. These technologies are posing new challenges to acquisitions. For example, according to U.S. Air

---

[28] Department of Defense, *Defense Acquisition Performance Assessment Report*, January 2006, p. 7.

[29] Office of the Under Secretary of Defense for Acquisition, Technology, and Logistics, Buying Commercial: *Gaining the Cost/Schedule Benefits for Defense Systems*, Defense Science Board Task Force on Integrating Commercial Systems into the DOD, Effectively and Efficiently, February 2009, p. xvii.

[30] Office of the Under Secretary of Defense For Acquisition, Technology, and Logistics, *Creating an Effective National Security Industrial Base for the 21st Century: An Action Plan to Address the Coming Crisis*, Defense Science Board Task Force on Defense Industrial Structure for Transformation, July 2008, p. 15. See also: Kenneth Flamm, "Post-Cold War Policy and the U.S. Defense Industrial Base," *National Academy of Engineering of the National Academies*, vol. 35, no. 1 (Spring 2005); Barry D. Watts, *Sustaining the U.S. Defense Industrial base as a Strategic Asset*, Center for Strategic and Budgetary Assessments, Backgrounder, September 2013, p. 15.

[31] Kenneth Flamm, "Post-Cold War Policy and the U.S. Defense Industrial Base," *National Academy of Engineering of the National Academies*, vol. 35, no. 1 (Spring 2005); See Business Executives for National Security, *Getting to Best: Reforming the Defense Acquisition Enterprise*, A Business Imperative for Change from the Task Force on Defense Acquisition Law and Oversight, July, 2009, p. 4.

[32] Data provided to CRS by Semiconductor Industry, October, 2013.

[33] Zachary Fryer-Biggs, "Looking Beyond Defense: Firms Grow Revenue—By Diversifying," *DefenseNews*, July 22, 2013, p. 11.

Force Lt. Gen. Christopher Bogdan, the biggest risk to the F-35 program is software development.[34] Some analysts believe that the increasing complexity of systems is the principal reason that aircraft development times have increased significantly since 1980.[35]

- *U.S. military spending is declining, squeezing acquisition accounts.* Constraints on U.S. defense spending, combined with real growth in per-capita expenditure for military personnel and pay benefits, limit the funding available for acquisitions and bring about reductions in force structure.[36] These effects also reduce potential economies of scale in defense production and can make it more difficult to pursue acquisitions associated with specialized or niche capabilities.

- *As U.S. military spending is declining, other countries are investing more in their militaries.* DOD obligated more money on just contracts in FY2012 ($360 billion) then the combined value of the five largest non-U.S. total defense budgets in the world ($335 billion).[37] Some analysts believe that given recent trends, the United States may not continue to dominate defense spending as much as it has in recent years. These analysts point to countries such as Russia and China. China's military modernization has been fueled by two decades of steadily increasing military spending. According to a DOD report to Congress, China's officially disclosed military budget increased an average of 9.7% annually in inflation-adjusted terms from 2003 to 2012.[38]

- *DOD-financed research and development is playing a less important role in innovation and development.[39]* DOD is spending a decreasing share of its contracting dollars on R&D contracts. In FY1998, 18% of DOD contract obligations were dedicated to R&D contracts compared to just 10% in FY2013 (see **Figure 3**). One analyst pointed out that even though the military is still an important funder of specific, leading-edge technologies such as supercomputers and microelectromechanical systems devices, "commercial demand for these products has far outstripped the requirements of the military."[40] At the same time, technologies developed for the commercial market are commonly adapted for military use. As one general officer stated, whereas the military used to go to industry and tell them to create a technology to meet a specific requirement,

---

[34] Andrea Shalal-Esa, "Pentagon Sees Some Risk of Delay in F-35 Software," *NBCnews.com*, April 24, 2013, at http://www.nbcnews.com/id/51649848/ns/technology_and_science-tech_and_gadgets/t/pentagon-sees-some-risk-delay-f—software/#.UlWMmm3zByU.

[35] Office of the Under Secretary of Defense Acquisition, Technology and Logistics, *Performance of the Defense Acquisition System*, 2013 Annual Report, June 28, 2013, p. 57. Aircraft development times have also markedly increased in the commercial aerospace market.

[36] Department of Defense, *Defense Budget Priorities and Choices*, Fiscal Year 2014, April 2013, p. 5.

[37] The five largest 2012 defense budgets were China ($102.4B), United Kingdom ($60.8B), Russia ($59.9B), Japan ($59.4B), and Saudi Arabia ($52.5B). Source: The International Institute for Strategic Studies, *The Military Balance 2013*, the annual assessment of global military capabilities and defence economics, London, 20113, p. 41.

[38] See CRS Report R41108, *U.S.-China Relations: An Overview of Policy Issues*, by Susan V. Lawrence, p. 16.

[39] See Business Executives for National Security, *Getting to Best: Reforming the Defense Acquisition Enterprise*, A Business Imperative for Change from the Task Force on Defense Acquisition Law and Oversight, July 2009, p. 4.

[40] Kenneth Flamm, "Post-Cold War Policy and the U.S. Defense Industrial Base," *National Academy of Engineering of the National Academies*, vol. 35, no. 1 (Spring 2005).

increasingly the military is going to industry and asking them to adapt an existing commercial technology to military requirements.[41]

Many analysts believe that the current acquisition system is not well suited to meet the challenges of an ever changing landscape and that fundamental reforms are necessary.[42] In 2009, Norman Augustine (former CEO of Lockheed Martin) and former Senators Gary Hart and Warren Rudman wrote that the defense acquisition system operates

> too slowly and at vastly greater cost than necessary. In earlier times we could arguably afford such flaws in efficiency, but we can afford them no longer.... We must examine the status quo systemically, in all its aspects, in order to make necessary and long overdue changes. If we do not, we will be in an increasingly sclerotic defense acquisition process that may one day no longer be able to supply American war fighters with the means to assure this nation's freedom and security.[43]

Now May Be a Good Time for Acquisition Reform

Historically, eras of budgetary restraint have been associated with the pursuit and implementation of acquisition reform. In the 1980s, the deficit targets enacted as part of the Gramm-Rudman-Hollings Act (The Balanced Budget and Emergency Deficit Control Act of 1985; P.L. 99-17) are seen by analysts as having contributed to development of the Packard Report and changes in defense acquisitions. Later, the Budget Enforcement Act of 1990 (Title X of The Omnibus Budget Reconciliation Act of 1990; P.L. 101-508) and related limits on defense spending are seen as having led to the Perry Report of 1994 and another round of far-reaching acquisition reform. Against the current backdrop of the Budget Control Act of 2011 (P.L. 112-25) and declines in defense spending, many analysts argue that the stage is set for a renewed effort to embark on a significant effort to improve defense acquisitions.

A number of analysts and DOD believe that recent changes within the military make significant reform possible. These officials and analysts suggest that a culture shift is occurring within the department—a shift that reflects a better understanding of the importance of defense acquisitions, more attention to fiscal discipline, and a fuller commitment on the part of senior leadership, uniform personnel, and civilian personnel to support efforts to improve defense acquisitions. Changes contributing to the culture shift include the following:

Operations in Iraq and Afghanistan have highlighted the importance of acquisitions. In the early years of the conflicts, contracting in Iraq and Afghanistan was done on an ad-hoc basis, without significant consideration of implications for foreign policy and without putting in place necessary

---

[41] Based on discussion with CRS analyst, May 8, 2013.

[42] Department of Defense, *Defense Acquisition Performance Assessment Report*, January 2006, p. 6; Business Executives for National Security, A Business Imperative for Change from the Task Force on Defense Acquisition Law and Oversight, July, 2009, p. 4. Then Secretary of Defense William Perry used the same logic to implement acquisition reforms in the 1990s. He stated "Because the world in which DoD now must operate has changed beyond the limits of the existing acquisition system's ability to adjust or evolve—the system must be totally re-engineered. If DoD is going to be capable of responding to the demands of the next decade, there must be a carefully planned, fundamental re-engineering or re-invention of each segment of the acquisition process." See Honorable William J. Perry, *Acquisition Reform: A Mandate for Change*, Department of Defense, February 9, 1994, p. 9; Department of Defense, *Defense Acquisition Performance Assessment Report*, January 2006, Introductory Letter by Chairman Ronald Kadish.

[43] Business Executives for National Security, *A Business Imperative for Change from the Task Force on Defense Acquisition Law and Oversight*, July, 2009, p. iii.

---

oversight systems. Insufficient resources were dedicated to oversight, resulting in poor performance, billions of dollars of waste, and failure to achieve mission goals.[44] However, the experiences of the operational force underscored the importance of acquisitions to senior leaders and prompted numerous internal efforts to examine contractor support, such as the report of the Commission on Army Acquisition and Program Management in Expeditionary Operations (known as the Gansler report).

Constrained budgets are fostering a culture of better decision making. Former Secretary of Defense Robert Gates stated that as a result of defense spending more than doubling between FY2001 and FY2010, "we've lost our ability to prioritize, to make hard decisions, to do tough analysis, to make trades."[45] As mentioned earlier, declines in defense acquisition spending since FY2008 have resulted in efforts to prioritize programs, reign in the 'gold-plating' of requirements, and increase the focus on costs.[46]

Data is improving.[47] Advances in information technology are making it possible to better track and analyze larger amounts of data. DOD is improving its information technology and business systems, and has embarked on a number of wide-ranging efforts to gather and analyze data to inform policy decisions, often at the behest of Congress. For example, the Weapon System Acquisition Reform Act of 2009 required DOD to conduct a root-cause analysis of the cost, schedule, and performance of Major Defense Acquisition Programs that experience cost growth that surpasses the thresholds set forth in the Nunn-McCurdy Act.[48] Over the years, these analyses have provided insight into what drives cost growth. Despite the progress being made, there continue to be significant gaps in the data available and in the reliability of some existing data.[49]

In sum, the unique combination of constrained budgets, a changing strategic and industrial landscape, recent experiences in Iraq and Afghanistan, and the increased availability of data have led many analysts and officials to conclude that this may be a unique opportunity to embark on another effort to improve defense acquisitions.[50]

---

[44] CRS Report R43074, *Department of Defense's Use of Contractors to Support Military Operations: Background, Analysis, and Issues for Congress*, by Moshe Schwartz.

[45] Department of Defense, "DOD News Briefing with Secretary Gates and Adm. Mullen from the Pentagon," press release, June 6, 2011, http://www.defense.gov/transcripts/transcript.aspx?transcriptid=4747.

[46] See Yamil Berard, "Former Pentagon leader says defense cuts are necessary," *Fort Worth Star-Telegram*, October 16, 2013.; Barry D. Watts, *Sustaining the U.S. Defense Industrial base as a Strategic Asset*, Center for Strategic and Budgetary Assessments, Backgrounder, September 2013, p. 15.

[47] Office of the Under Secretary of Defense Acquisition, Technology and Logistics, *Performance of the Defense Acquisition System*, 2013 Annual Report, June 28, 2013, p. 106.

[48] P.L. 111-23, Section 103. The Nunn-McCurdy Act requires DOD to report to Congress whenever a major defense acquisition program experiences cost overruns that exceed certain cost thresholds. See CRS Report R41293, *The Nunn-McCurdy Act: Background, Analysis, and Issues for Congress*, by Moshe Schwartz.

[49] Office of the Under Secretary of Defense Acquisition, Technology and Logistics, *Performance of the Defense Acquisition System*, 2013 Annual Report, June 28, 2013, p. 105; U.S. Army, *Army Strong: Equipped, Trained and Ready*, Final Report of the 2010 Army Acquisition Review, January 11, 2011, p. iv. The report found that "The Army lacks a sufficiently robust and trustworthy database on acquisition programs, workforce and lessons learned," p. 42.

[50] Bill Greenwalt, "Once More Unto The Breach, This Time For Acquisition Reform," *Breaking Defense*, April 23, 2014. At http://breakingdefense.com/2014/04/once-more-unto-the-breach-this-time-for-acquisition-reform/.

Recent DOD Efforts to Improve Acquisitions

In recent years, DOD has taken a number of steps to improve the process by which it buys goods and services. At a press conference in May 2009, then Secretary of Defense Robert Gates announced steps to rein in cost and schedule growth in weapon system acquisitions.[51] He called for cancelling programs that significantly exceed budget, do not meet current military needs, or do not have sufficiently mature technology. Addressing programs with significant cost growth, he called for the cancellation of a number of programs, including the VH-71 presidential helicopter. He also called for the cancellation of programs for which a strong requirement no longer existed or for which needed technology had not matured—such as the ground components of the Future Combat System and missile defense's Multiple Kill Vehicle (MKV). Other programs, such as the F-22 and Air Force Combat Search and Rescue X (CSAR-X), were also cancelled or curtailed.

That same year, Secretary Gates also sought to improve the use of contractors during military operations. He acknowledged DOD's failure to adequately prepare for the use of contractors when he testified that the use of contractors occurred

> without any supervision or without any coherent strategy on how we were going to do it and without conscious decisions about what we will allow contractors to do and what we won't allow contractors to do... We have not thought holistically or coherently about our use of contractors, particularly when it comes to combat environments or combat training.[52]

Since that time, DOD has taken steps to improve how it uses contractors during operations,[53] such as establishing a Functional Capabilities Integration Board, co-chaired by the Deputy Assistant Secretary of Defense for Program Support and the Joint Staff Vice Director of Logistics. This board is a forum for senior leaders to come together to address critical operational contract support issues.[54] DOD has also significantly expanded regulation, policy, doctrine, and training related to operational contract support, including the following examples:

- In 2009, DOD released a directive entitled, *Orchestrating, Synchronizing, and Integrating Program Management of Contingency Acquisition Planning and its Operational Execution.*[55]

- In 2010, DOD updated its *Policy and Procedures for Determining Workforce Mix*, which addressed contractor personnel as part of the total force.[56]

---

[51] For the full text of the press conference, see http://www.defense.gov/transcripts/transcript.aspx?transcriptid=4396.

[52] U.S. Congress, Senate Committee on Armed Services, *To Receive Testimony on the Challenges Facing the Department of Defense*, 110th Cong., 2nd sess., January 27, 2009.

[53] U.S. Government Accountability Office, *Warfighter Support: DOD Needs Additional Steps to Fully Integrate Operational Contract Support into Contingency Planning*, GAO-13-212, February 8, 2013, p. 3.

[54] The Operational Contract Support Functional Capabilities Integration Board was chartered based on the authority set forth in Section 854 of the John Warner National Defense Authorization Act for 2007 (P.L. 109-364). See http://www.acq.osd mil/log/PS/fcib html.

[55] DOD Directive 3020.49 *Orchestrating, Synchronizing, and Integrating Program Management of Contingency Acquisition Planning and its Operational Execution*, March 2009.

[56] DOD Instruction 1100.22, *Policy and Procedures for Determining Workforce Mix*, April 2010. DOD is in the process of updating DOD Instruction 1100.22 as well as DOD Directive 1100.4, *Guidance for Manpower Management*.

- In 2011, a major update to the DOD Instruction for operational contract support was released, which established roles and responsibilities for managing operational contract support.[57]

- In 2012, DOD updated its joint planning and execution policy to include operational contract support in many non-logistical functional areas, such as intelligence, personnel, and engineering.[58]

- In 2013, DOD developed standards for using private security contractors.[59]

- In 2014, DOD conducted a joint exercise for operational contract support.[60]

In addition to steps taken to improve discrete areas of defense acquisitions, such as weapon systems and contingency contracting, DOD has embarked on a comprehensive effort to improve the overall defense acquisition system. Many of these initiatives can be traced back to the ideas and recommendations of the Packard Report. The current effort generally focuses on

- rewriting the rules and regulations to create a more efficient and effective acquisition process;

- improving the culture and professionalism of the acquisition workforce; and

- improving the overall performance of the acquisition system.

On September 14, 2010, then-Under Secretary of Defense for Acquisition, Technology and Logistics Ashton Carter issued the memorandum *Better Buying Power: Guidance for Obtaining Greater Efficiency and Productivity in Defense Spending*. The memorandum outlined 23 principal actions to improve efficiency, including making affordability a requirement, increasing competition, and decreasing the time it takes to acquire a system. In November 2012, Secretary Carter's successor, Frank Kendall, launched the Better Buying Power 2.0 initiative, an update to the original Better Buying Power effort, aimed at "implementing practices and policies designed to improve the productivity of the Department of Defense and of the industrial base that provides the products and services" to the warfighters.[61] Better Buying Power 2.0 contained 34 separate initiatives, including reducing the frequency of senior-level reviews and improving requirements and market research.[62] According to officials, Better Buying Power 3.0 is in development.

---

[57] DOD Instruction 3020.41, *Operational Contract Support*, December 2011. In 2012, this Instruction was codified in 32 Code of Federal Regulations Part 158.

[58] Chairman of the Joint Chiefs of Staff Manual 3130.03, *Adaptive Planning and Execution (APEX) Planning Formats and Guidance*, October 2012.

[59] Private Security Contractor standards were required by Section 833 of the NDAA for FY2011. The American National Standards Institute validated these standards in March 2013.

[60] The exercise has been held annually for the past four years. The 2014 exercise, the first to be sponsored by the Joint Chiefs of Staff, was attended by some 500 individuals drawn from across military services and components.

[61] While much of the original effort remains intact, the new version does contain some changes. For example, the original effort called for increased use of fixed-price contracts whereas the newer version emphasizes the use of an appropriate contract type, depending on the circumstances. Quote taken from document provided to CRS by DOD entitled *Better Buying Power (BBP) 2.0 Summary*.

[62] The full text of the *Better Buying Power 2.0* memorandum can be downloaded at http://bbp.dau mil/doc/USD-ATL%20Memo%2024Apr13%20-%20BBP%202.0%20Implementation%20Directive.pdf.

DOD has also undertaken a comprehensive effort to overhaul the regulatory structure that governs defense acquisitions.[63] For example:

- On January 10, 2012, DOD issued updated versions of the instructions *Charter of the Joint Requirements Oversight Council* and *Joint Capabilities Integration and Development System.*

- On January 19, 2012, DOD issued an updated version of the *Manual for the Operation of the Joint Capabilities Integration and Development System.*[64]

- On January 25, 2013, DOD issued an updated version of the directive *The Planning, Programming, and Budgeting System (PPBS).*

- On November 26, 2013, DOD issued an updated "interim" instruction *Operation of the Defense Acquisition System* (5000.02).

- On December 2, 2013, Secretary Kendall announced the establishment of a team to develop a legislative proposal that would attempt to "simplify the existing body of law and replace it with a more coherent and 'user friendly' set of requirements, without sacrificing the intention behind existing statutes."[65]

These updates focus on fostering a culture that provides more autonomy to the workforce and an emphasis on making good management decisions instead of managing by compliance or a check-the-box mentality. For example, the new DOD Instruction 5000.02 (*Operation of the Defense Acquisition System*) emphasizes that

> the structure of a DOD acquisition program and the procedures used should be tailored as much as possible to the characteristics of the product being acquired, and to the totality of circumstances associated with the program....[66]

In promoting a more tailored approach, the instruction goes on to outline four different models (and two additional hybrid models) for acquisitions, depending on the type of program being pursued. This theme of good decision-making is repeated in numerous documents, speeches, and policy decisions, including the following examples:

1. In the memorandum issued to implement the Better Buying Power (BBP) 2.0 initiative, Secretary Kendall wrote "the first responsibility of the acquisition workforce is to think. We need to be true professionals who apply our education, training, and experience through analysis and creative, informed thought to address our daily decisions. Our workforce should be encouraged by leaders to think and not to automatically default to a perceived 'school solution' just

---

[63] See memo accompanying issuance of interim DOD Instruction 5000.02, Deputy Secretary of Defense Ashton Carter, *Defense Acquisition*, Department of Defense, November 26, 2013.

[64] The manual can be found at https://dap.dau mil/policy/Documents/2012/ JCIDS%20Manual%2019%20Jan%202012.pdf. A four page errata sheet was issued on September 20, 2012 (see https://dap.dau mil/policy/Documents/2012/JCIDS%20Manual%20Errata%20-%2020%20Sept%202012.pdf).

[65] Under Secretary of Defense Frank Kendall, *The New Department of Defense Instruction 5000.02*, Department of Defense, Memorandum for the Acquisition Workforce, December 2, 2013, p. 1.

[66] Department of Defense, Instruction 5000.02, *Operation of the Defense Acquisition System*, p. 3, November 25, 2013.

because it is expected to be approved more easily. BBP 2.0, like BBP 1.0, is not rigid dogma—it is guidance subject to professional judgment."[67]

2. A memorandum jointly issued by Under Secretaries of Defense Robert Hale (comptroller) and Kendall stated "the threat that funding will be taken away or that future budgets can be reduced unless funds are obligated on schedule is a strong and perverse motivator. We risk creating incentives to enter into quick but poor business deals or to expend funds primarily to avoid reductions in future budget years. We need to rethink how we approach managing mid-year and end-of-year obligations and to change the types of behavior we reward or punish."[68]

3. There has been a significant focus on using data to drive decisions. Evidence of this shift includes a sign hanging by the door of Secretary Kendall's office which reads "In God We Trust. All Others Must Bring Data"[69] and the release of the first annual report *Performance of the Defense Acquisitions System*, which relies extensively on data gathered over 30 years to analyze and measure the effectiveness of weapon system acquisitions.[70] The annual report is one of, if not the most, comprehensive, data-driven analyses on defense acquisitions issued by DOD in many years.[71]

Many members of the acquisition workforce have argued that these efforts, while laudable, have generally not had a significant impact on defense acquisitions. These individuals point out that the fundamental incentives in the acquisition system remain unaltered.[72] For example, they say, there is a culture within DOD (and other agencies) that encourages the obligation of funds before they expire out of fear that if money is not spent, future budgets will be cut. This belief, which may be reinforced by certain congressional oversight practices,[73] encourages managers to prioritize spending based on an arbitrary calendar deadline instead of sound business decisions.[74] According to this argument, reform efforts will have only limited impact until incentives are changed to better align with desired outcomes. Others have argued that implementing such far-reaching change takes years of sustained effort and that the groundwork is being set for long-term change that may not produce visible gains for years to come.

---

[67] Under Secretary of Defense Frank Kendall, *Implementation Directive for Better Buying Power 2.0 - Achieving Greater Efficiency and Productivity in Defense Spending*, Department of Defense, April 24, 2013, p. 1.

[68] Under Secretary of Defense Robert Hale and Under Secretary of Defense Frank Kendall, *Department of Defense Management of Unobligated Funds; Obligation Rate Tenets*, Office of the Secretary of Defense, September 10, 2012, p. 1.

[69] Quote attributed to W. Edwards Deming.

[70] Office of the Under Secretary of Defense, Acquisition, Technology and Logistics, *Performance of the Defense Acquisition System*, 2013 Annual Report, June 28, 2013. The concluding comments of the report states "measuring the performance of defense acquisition provides objective, quantitative information on our current performance. The following insights provide some broader perspectives and considerations. These should inform and enable stable improvement in our overall acquisition performance." p. 109.

[71] The report acknowledges that more work and more data analysis needs to be done; the report seeks to provide initial results in what is expected to be a long-range effort to use data to inform efforts to improve acquisitions.

[72] Based on dozens of CRS interviews with acquisition personnel from June 2013-May 2014.

[73] DOD briefings on acquisition programs, apparently at the request of some Congressional recipients, routinely conclude with slides providing data on percentages of prior-year funding obligated and expended to date.

[74] Robert F. Hale and Frank Kendall, *Department of Defense Management of Unobligated Funds; Obligations Tenets*, Office of the Secretary of Defense, Memorandum, September 10, 2012.

A number of analysts, industry officials, and DOD officials argue that constrained budgets are the key to fostering a culture of better decision-making. Some analysts argue that declines in defense acquisition spending since FY2008 have resulted in efforts to prioritize programs, rein in the expansion of requirements, improve efficiency, and increase the focus on costs.[75]

Some analysts suggest that DOD does not have the authority or ability to substantially improve the acquisition process on its own and that substantial reform requires close, consistent, and long-term collaboration between DOD, Congress, and industry. For example, a comprehensive effort to streamline and improve the efficiency of the acquisition regulations will in some instances require Congress to amend existing legislation, DOD to amend internal practices, and industry to play a constructive role.

Issues for Congress

What DOD can do on its own to improve acquisitions can only go so far—for more extensive reforms, DOD needs help from Congress. Such efforts as the Goldwater-Nichols Act, establishment of the Federal Acquisition Regulation, creation of Defense Acquisition University, and streamlined acquisition rules and regulations were all the result of congressional action. More recently, many analysts and senior DOD officials have stated that without the efforts of Congress, DOD would not have been as successful at improving operational contract support.[76] As a 2009 report by the Business Executives for National Security argues, Congress "sets the expectations and tone for the entire [defense] enterprise—and must be at the forefront of any change."[77] The role of Congress may be particularly important in the area of workforce and culture. As GAO stated as far back as 1992, "ultimately, change will occur only through the collective action of acquisition participants, particularly within the Department of Defense and the Congress, for it is their actions that dictate the incentives that drive the process."[78]

Improving the Workforce

Despite the hundreds of recommendations to improve defense acquisitions, most reports seeking to address the fundamental weaknesses of the system arrive at the same conclusion: the key to good acquisitions is having a good workforce and giving them the resources, incentives, and authority to do their job.[79] As David Packard wrote in a 1986 report to President Reagan,

---

[75] See Yamil Berard, "Former Pentagon leader says defense cuts are necessary," *Fort Worth Star-Telegram*, October 16, 2013; Barry D. Watts, *Sustaining the U.S. Defense Industrial base as a Strategic Asset*, Center for Strategic and Budgetary Assessments, Backgrounder, September 2013, p. 15.

[76] See CRS Report R43074, *Department of Defense's Use of Contractors to Support Military Operations: Background, Analysis, and Issues for Congress*, by Moshe Schwartz.

[77] Business Executives for National Security, *Getting to Best: Reforming the Defense Acquisition Enterprise*, A Business Imperative for Change from the Task Force on Defense Acquisition Law and Oversight, July, 2009, p. 12.

[78] U.S. General Accounting Office, *Weapons Acquisition: A Rare Opportunity for Lasting Change*, NSIAD 93-15, December 1992, p. 3.

[79] For additional discussions, see Thomas Christie, "Sound Policy, Awful Execution," *DefenseNews*, December 15, 2008, p. 53. Thomas Miller, "Rearranging Deck Chairs on the Titanic: Why Does Acquisition Reform Never Work?" *Defense AT&L*, November-December 2010, p. 27; Scott Reynolds, "Let's Fix It: A Five-Step Plan for Improving Acquisitions," *Defense AT&L*, November-December 2009, p. 18.

> Excellence in defense management cannot be achieved by the numerous management layers, large staffs, and countless regulations in place today. It depends ... on reducing all of these by adhering closely to basic, common sense principles: giving a few capable people the authority and responsibility to do their job, maintaining short lines of communication, and holding people accountable for results.[80]

A number of analysts have argued that the successive waves of acquisition reform have generally yielded limited results, due in large part to poor workforce management. As one recent analysis stated, "There is little doubt that acquisition reforms produce limited positive effects because they have not changed the basic incentives or pressures that drive the behavior of the participants in the acquisition process."[81] The workforce is not the only area that analysts believe needs to be improved—recommendations are aimed at budgeting, developing requirements, estimating costs, and other structural problems. However, without a culture that promotes good acquisition decisions, analysts believe that reform efforts will not achieve their fullest potential. This culture includes not only the acquisition workforce but also other people involved in the process, such as those who develop requirements and budgets. As Robert Hale wrote in 2002

> Efficiency requires change, and change is difficult to implement in any organization—public or private. To have any chance of success, there must be an incentive to change. Incentives start with the climate created by top leaders... But commitment must extend beyond the senior leadership to the Defense Department's field commanders and managers. Efficiencies achieved at the base or installation level could add up to substantial savings, and the individuals running these bases will be more likely to implement changes if they have incentives to do so.[82]

---

[80] *A Quest for Excellence*, Final Report to the President by the Blue Ribbon Commission of Defense Management, June 30, 1986.

[81] J. Ronald Fox, *Defense Acquisition Reform 1960-2009: An Elusive Goal* (Center of Military History, 2011), p. 190. This point was reiterated in Secretary Kendall's guidance on implementing the Better Buying Power initiatives, which stated "Policies and processes are of little use without acquisition professionals who are experienced, trained, and empowered to apply them effectively. At the end of the day, qualified people are essential to successful outcomes and professionalism, particularly in acquisition leaders, drives results more than any policy change." See Frank Kendall, *Implementation Directive for Better Buying Power 2.0 - Achieving Greater Efficiency and Productivity in Defense Spending*, Office of the Under Secretary of Defense Acquisition, Technology and Logistics, Memorandum, April 24, 2013.

[82] Robert F. Hale, *Promoting Efficiency in the Department of Defense: Keep Trying, Be Realistic*, Center for Strategic and Budgetary Assessments, January 2002, p. 20.

The Importance of People and Proper Incentives

Numerous reports have highlighted the importance of people in successful acquisitions. Below are conclusions from some of the most influential reports on defense acquisitions from 1970 to the present.

- "Regardless of how effective the overall system of Department procurement regulations may be judged to be, the key determinants of the ultimate effectiveness and efficiency of the Defense Procurement process are the procurement personnel.... The importance of this truism has not been appropriately reflected in the recruitment, career development, training, and management of the procurement workforce."[83] *Fitzhugh Report (1970)*

- "DOD must be able to attract, retain, and motivate well qualified acquisition personnel."[84] *Packard Report (1986)*

- "Making fundamental improvements in acquisitions will require attacking the cultural dimension of the problem. Changes of the type needed will not come easily. They must be directed at the system of incentives."[85] *GAO (1992)*

- "Give line managers more authority and accountability (reward results, not just compliance with rules; focus on the customer)."[86] *Perry Report (1994)*

- "The department should focus on creating incentives so that commanders and managers seek efficiencies."[87] *Robert Hale (2002)*

- "To repeat: the emphasis must be on the individuals in line management.... the key to effective execution of any contract is not the quality of the contract, it is the quality of the program management responding to clear assignment of authority and accountability for each program."[88] *QDR Independent Panel (2010)*

- "There is little doubt that acquisition reforms produce limited, positive effects because they have not changed the basic incentives or pressures that drive the behavior of the participants in the acquisition process."[89] *Defense Acquisition Reform: 1960-2009 (2011)*

Building a Capable, Trained, and Sufficiently Sized Workforce

Analysts have concluded that insufficient resources or shortages in the number of properly trained, sufficiently talented acquisition personnel increase the risk of poor contract performance, which in turn can lead to waste, fraud, and abuse.[90] In an effort to improve the size and quality of

---

[83] Department of Defense, *Report to the President and the Secretary of Defense on the Department of Defense by the Blue Ribbon Panel*, July 1, 1970, p. 94.

[84] *A Quest for Excellence*, Final Report to the President by the Blue Ribbon Commission of Defense Management, June 30, 1986, p. xxv.

[85] U.S. General Accounting Office, *Weapons Acquisition: A Rare Opportunity for Lasting Change*, NSIAD 93-15, December 1992, pp. 2-3.

[86] Honorable William J. Perry, *Acquisition Reform: A Mandate for Change*, Department of Defense, February 9, 1994, p. 9.

[87] Robert F. Hale, *Promoting Efficiency in the Department of Defense: Keep Trying, Be Realistic*, Center for Strategic and Budgetary Assessments, January 2002, p. iii.

[88] U.S. Institute for Peace, *The QDR in Perspective: Meeting America's National Security Needs in the 21st Century*, Final Report of the Quadrennial Defense Review Independent Panel, July 28, 2010, p. 86.

[89] J. Ronald Fox, *Defense Acquisition Reform 1960-2009: An Elusive Goal* (Center of Military History, 2011), p. 190.

[90] J. Ronald Fox, *Defense Acquisition Reform 1960-2009: An Elusive Goal* (Center of Military History, 2011), p. 195, 199. See also, Commission on Wartime Contracting in Iraq and Afghanistan, *At What Risk? Correcting over-reliance on contractors in contingency operations*, Second Interim Report to Congress, February 24, 2011, p. 17; United States Institute of Peace, *The QDR in Perspective: Meeting America's National Security Needs in the 21st Century*, 2010, p. 39; U.S. Government Accountability Office, *Military Operations: High-Level DOD Action Needed to Address Long-standing Problems with Management and Oversight of Contractors Supporting Deployed Forces*, GAO-07-145, (continued...)

the acquisition workforce, the FY2008 NDAA mandated the establishment of the Department of Defense Acquisition Workforce Fund to enable the "recruitment, training, and retention of acquisition personnel."[91] From FY2008 through FY2012, DOD obligated $2.3 billion through the fund. According to DOD, this funding was used to augment training and hire an additional 8,300 people in contracting, cost estimating, systems engineering, auditing, and other related fields. However, many analysts believe that while DOD and congressional efforts are starting to have a positive impact on the acquisition workforce, additional support and focus is needed.[92]

Creating the Right Incentives

Many analysts argue that even with a sufficiently robust, highly trained and capable workforce, effective acquisition reform depends on having the right incentive structure in place. Some argue that practices proven effective in the private sector have not been similarly effective when applied to government because the same incentives that made the practice effective in industry are not present in government.

Often, the incentives in the acquisition process, analysts argue, encourage people to make poor decisions.[93] One example, discussed above, is the incentive to obligate funds before the end of the fiscal year. Another example of incentives driving poor acquisition decisions relates to cost estimating. Senior defense officials, both past and current, acknowledge that program advocates have strong incentives to underestimate program acquisition costs. Contractors use low cost estimates to win the contract; program representatives use low estimates to argue for approval of the system against competing systems.[94] In 1981, then-Deputy Secretary of Defense Frank C. Carlucci testified that low cost estimates "are fueled by optimistic contractor proposals to win competitions and program managers who want to see their programs funded."[95] Almost 30 years later, then-Under Secretary of Defense for Acquisition, Technology, and Logistics John Young echoed this sentiment, stating "the enterprise will often pressure acquisition teams and industry to provide low, optimistic estimates to help start programs."[96]

(continued)

December 18, 2006; Commission on Wartime Contracting In Iraq and Afghanistan, *Transforming Wartime Contracting: Controlling costs, reducing risk*, Final Report to Congress, August, 2011, pp. 83-84; Business Executives for National Security, *Getting to Best: Reforming the Defense Acquisition Enterprise*, A Business Imperative for Change from the Task Force on Defense Acquisition Law and Oversight, July, 2009, p. 3.

[91] P.L. 110-181, Section 852.

[92] Data provided by DOD. See also Department of Defense, *Defense Acquisition Workforce Development Fund (DAWDF) FY2012 Report to Congress*, Department of Defense, April 2013, p. 4. DOD has recognized the need to dedicate sufficient resources to develop a more professional and skilled workforce. The 2010 Quadrennial Defense Review states that "to operate effectively, the acquisition system must be supported by an appropriately sized cadre of acquisition professionals with the right skills and training to successfully perform their jobs.... We will continue to significantly enhance training and retention programs in order to bolster the capability and size of the acquisition workforce." pp. 77-78.

[93] J. Ronald Fox, *Defense Acquisition Reform 1960-2009: An Elusive Goal* (Center of Military History, 2011), pp. 197-199; Department of Defense, *Defense Acquisition Performance Assessment Report*, January 2006, p. 5; See Business Executives for National Security, *Getting to Best: Reforming the Defense Acquisition Enterprise*, A Business Imperative for Change from the Task Force on Defense Acquisition Law and Oversight, July, 2009, p. 3.

[94] House Armed Services Hearings, 97th Cong., 1st Sess., Volume 11, 1981. Op. Cit. p. 883.

[95] House Armed Services Hearings, 97th Cong., 1st Sess., Volume 11, 1981. Op. Cit. p. 1086.

[96] John J. Young, Jr., *Reasons for Cost Changes for Selected Major Defense Acquisition Programs (MDAPs)*, Memorandum, January 30, 2009.

The absence of more reliable cost estimates prevents Congress from deciding on competing strategic and budget priorities based on realistic cost assumptions and hinders DOD from developing a well-conceived acquisition plan. The 2010 Quadrennial Defense Review stated, "our system of defining requirements and developing capability too often encourages reliance on overly optimistic cost estimates. In order for the Pentagon to produce weapons systems efficiently, it is critical to have budget stability—but it is impossible to attain such stability in DOD's modernization budgets if we continue to underestimate the cost of such systems from the start."[97]

Establishing Authority and Accountability

Authority and accountability are viewed as critical elements in building an effective workforce.[98] Without authority, even the most skilled and incentivized professionals cannot effectively run and manage a program. Yet many analysts believe that the management structure is too bureaucratic and that too many people can say "no" or influence a program. As one program manager recently quipped, the inside joke among program managers is that "We are not really sure who runs the program."[99] Without anyone having practical authority to manage a program, there is no one who can effectively be held accountable. The Quadrennial Defense Review Independent Panel concluded that "the fundamental reason for the continued underperformance in acquisition activities is *fragmentation of authority and accountability for performance.*"[100]

Congress could consider workforce as an area ripe for acquisition reform. In considering the workforce, issues for Congress can include the extent to which

- the rules and regulations governing workforce management (including hiring, firing, promotion and retention authorities) promote or inhibit DOD's ability to effectively hire and retain capable people, and promote accountability;

- key personnel are endowed with appropriate authority and given sufficient resources to most effectively manage programs;

- the incentives inherent in the rules and regulations governing the acquisition process promote or inhibit efficient and effective acquisitions management; and

- DOD has and is effectively implementing a strategic plan to build, develop, and manage the acquisition workforce (at the military service and OSD level).

---

[97] Department of Defense, Quadrennial Defense Review Report, February 2010, p. 76.

[98] The Packard Report, for example, stated "We must give acquisition personnel more authority to do their jobs. If we make it possible for people to do the right thing the first time and allow them to use their common sense, then we believe that the Department can get by with far fewer people." See p. xxiv.

[99] Based on conversations with program managers and other acquisition personnel, September 14, 2013.

[100] U.S. Institute for Peace, *The QDR in Perspective: Meeting America's National Security Needs in the 21st Century*, Final Report of the Quadrennial Defense Review Independent Panel, July 28, 2010, p. 85. Italics as in original.

Targeted Reform Efforts

In addition to workforce management, efforts to reform specific areas of defense acquisitions, as was done by the Weapon System Acquisition Reform Act of 2009 and efforts to improve Operational Contract Support, have the potential to generate cost savings and operational benefits. Examples of possible areas ripe for reform include streamlining acquisition laws and regulations, and focusing on contract logistics.

Streamlining Acquisition Laws and Regulations

In some instances, regulations aimed at improving the acquisition process or promoting public-policy goals impose unintended cost or regulatory burdens to industry. A number of analysts have argued that repealing or amending regulations that no longer provide a substantial benefit could simplify the acquisition process, remove unnecessary regulatory burdens on industry, and entice more companies to compete for defense and other federal government contracts (see **Appendix A** for a more detailed discussion of the complexity of the acquisition process). Sometimes, the laws and regulations governing defense procurement can add to the cost of doing business, as in the case of certain domestic source restrictions like the Berry Amendment. Such a perspective does not necessarily argue for wholesale removal of regulations and oversight, but rather an approach of weighing the costs to industry and government against the policy and oversight benefits of certain regulations.[101] Congress could also choose to amend statutes and regulations so as to alleviate regulatory or financial burdens while preserving the intent of the regulation.

Congress has spearheaded past efforts to streamline the laws and regulations governing acquisitions. For example, Section 800 of the FY1991 NDAA[102] required the Under Secretary of Defense for Acquisition to establish an advisory panel charged with reviewing the acquisition laws applicable to the Department of Defense.[103] This effort ultimately resulted in enactment of the Federal Acquisition Streamlining Act of 1994,[104] which was a comprehensive reform effort.

Logistics and Supply Chain Management

Some government officials and industry experts have identified logistics as an area where significant cost savings could be generated without negatively affecting operational

---

[101] Honorable William J. Perry, *Acquisition Reform*, Department of Defense, A Mandate for Change, February 9, 1994, p. 8.

[102] P.L. 101-510

[103] The panel was directed to

> (1) review the acquisition laws applicable to the Department of Defense with a view toward streamlining the defense acquisition process;
>
> (2) make any recommendations for the repeal or amendment of such laws that the panel considers necessary, as a result of such review, to—
>> (A) eliminate any such laws that are unnecessary for the establishment and administration of buyer and seller relationships in procurement;
>> (B) ensure the continuing financial and ethical integrity of defense procurement programs; and
>> (C) protect the best interests of the Department of Defense; and
>
> (3) prepare a proposed code of relevant acquisition laws.

[104] P.L. 103-155.

---

capabilities.[105] Recent reports have identified instances of wasteful spending in this area. For example, the DOD Inspector General has developed a body of work that found the following:

- Boeing charged the Army about $13 million more than fair and reasonable prices for 18 parts on a support contract.[106]

- Sikorsky charged the Army approximately $12 million more than fair and reasonable prices for 28 parts.[107]

- Boeing charged DLA Aviation $13.7 million more than fair and reasonable prices for 27 parts associated with 1,469 delivery orders.[108]

In addition, the Special Inspector General for Afghan Reconstruction reported that military forces in Afghanistan were unable to account for about $230 million worth of spare parts and then ordered $138 million of additional parts without sufficient accountability.[109]

Given the examples of potential savings identified to date, Congress could consider logistics and supply chain management as a potential area for increased congressional oversight and further investigation.

---

[105] Based on conversations with CRS analysts, July 2013 through October 2013.

[106] Department of Defense Inspector General, "Excess Inventory and Contract Pricing Problems Jeopardize the Army Contract with Boeing to Support the Corpus Christi Army Depot," Report D-2011-061, May 3, 2011.

[107] Department of Defense Inspector General, "Pricing and Escalation Issues Weaken the Effectiveness of the Army Contract with Sikorsky to Support the Corpus Christi Army Depot," Report D-2011-104, September 8, 2011,

[108] Department of Defense Inspector General, "Improved Guidance Needed to Obtain Fair and Reasonable Prices for Sole-Source Spare Parts Procured by the Defense Logistics Agency from the Boeing Company," Report DODIG-2013-090, June 7, 2013,

[109] Special Inspector General for Afghanistan Reconstruction, Afghan National Army: Combined Security Transition Command-Afghanistan Lacks Key Information on Inventory in Stock and Requirements for Vehicle Spare Parts, SIGAR 14-3, October 16, 2013, p. 1.

Appendix A. Complexity of the Acquisition Process

Until World War II, the regulations and rules governing government contracting in general, and defense contracting in particular, were minimal. After World War II, the growth in defense acquisition regulations was so rapid and uncoordinated that an Office of Federal Procurement Policy study from the late 1970s found that DOD had 79 different offices issuing procurement regulations and that these offices had developed a procurement process that consisted of some 30,000 pages of regulations.

Concerned that the defense acquisitions process was overly complex and unwieldy, Congress enacted the Federal Acquisition Streamlining Act of 1994[110] to overhaul the process. Despite this act and other congressional and executive branch efforts, contracting with the federal government remains a highly regulated process governed by a myriad of statutes and regulations.[111] These regulations govern such issues as

- how DOD solicits, negotiates, and awards a contract;

- what costs DOD will reimburse and how contractors account for those costs;

- the information systems used by contractors; and

- how contractors must comply with such rules as combatting trafficking in persons, maintaining a drug-free workplace, and other public policy goals.[112]

Factors contributing to the increased complexity of the acquisition system include past reform efforts, increased complexity of technology and weapon systems, and inclusion of public policy goals into the acquisition process. Examples of regulations that reflect public policy goals include the requirement to purchase certain goods from domestic suppliers (such as the Berry Amendment and Buy American Act),[113] preferences for buying goods and services in Afghanistan to support campaign objectives in theatre, requirements to take steps to combat trafficking in persons,[114] set asides to promote small businesses and other entities perceived as disadvantaged, and the International Traffic in Arms Regulations.

In some instances, conflicts arise between obtaining the best value for the government and promoting public policy goals. Some analysts debate the value of regulations requiring certain defense items to be manufactured domestically. Others argue these requirements are necessary to ensure domestic sources of supply during war time. Some analysts argue domestic sourcing regulations unnecessarily increase the cost to government, that the regulations could be implemented in a more cost-efficient manner, and that some items are on the list for protectionist reasons, not to preserve military capabilities.

---

[110] P.L. 103-155.

[111] http://www.cdc.gov/od/pgo/funding/contracts/contractmain.shtm.

[112] Carl L. Vacketta, *Federal Government Contract Overview,* http://library findlaw.com/1999/Jan/1/241470 html.

[113] See DFARS, Part 225.7002; FAR Part 25. See also CRS Report RL31236, *The Berry Amendment: Requiring Defense Procurement to Come from Domestic Sources,* by Valerie Bailey Grasso.

[114] FAR Subpart 22.17, Combating Trafficking in Persons.

The complexity of the regulations can make it difficult for some companies to enter the government contracting arena.[115] Many analysts believe that the rules and regulations governing defense acquisitions need to be further streamlined and simplified in a manner that reduces the burden on private industry and controls the increase in costs while preserving sufficient oversight.

---

[115] Ibid. See also Grant Thornton, 16th Annual Government Contractor Industry Survey Highlights Book, Industry Survey Highlights 2010, p. 7.

Appendix B. Constantly Changing Acquisition Rules

Some analysts believe that the successive reform efforts have discouraged some companies from seeking government contracts out of concern that the rules could be changed in the middle of the game. Implementing successive changes to the acquisition system can also add to the cost of doing business with DOD and make it more difficult for DOD and Congress to determine whether individual changes are having a positive or negative effect on the acquisition process.

Changes to the rules governing defense acquisitions generally are the result of legislation or executive branch rules and regulations.

Legislative Changes

In recent years, the primary mechanism by which Congress has exercised its legislative powers to reform defense acquisitions has been the annual National Defense Authorization Act (NDAA). Sections of these acts have prescribed requirements applicable to both specific acquisition programs and the acquisition structure overall, the latter of which has typically been addressed in Title VIII, which is usually called "Acquisition Policy, Acquisition Management, and Related Matters." Over a recent six-year period, the Title in the NDAA dealing with acquisitions included more than 275 sections.[116]

Other titles within the NDAA can also include legislation that affects companies seeking to contract with DOD.[117] At times, Congress has chosen to enact legislation affecting defense acquisitions in a stand-alone bill. For example, in May 2009, Congress passed and the President signed into law the Weapon Systems Acquisition Reform Act of 2009 (S. 454/P.L. 111-23), which contained a number of sections that impacted defense acquisitions, ranging from issues related to competition to conflicts of interest.

Regulatory Changes

DOD procurement activities are generally governed by three sets of federal government regulations:

- The first set of regulations, which applies to the entire federal government (including DOD unless stated otherwise), are found in the Federal Acquisition Regulation (FAR),

- The second set of regulations applies only to DOD and is found in the Defense Federal Acquisition Regulation Supplement, and

---

[116] Based on CRS review of the National Defense Authorization Acts for FY2008-2012. Not all sections in the Title impact private industry; rather, the volume of sections portrays the challenges in keeping abreast of legislative changes that could significantly impact industry.

[117] For example, the FY2010 NDAA, Title III (*Operation and Maintenance*) included a section effecting defense acquisitions. See P.L. 111-84, Sec. 325.

- The third set of regulations applies only to individual DOD components and is found in component-unique FAR Supplements.[118]

Procurement actions in DOD must adhere to the various regulations, and program managers must take the regulations into account during the planning and execution of their programs. The rules and regulations governing defense acquisitions can change at a rapid pace. For example, the DOD Directive 5000 series was established in 1971 to regulate the acquisition of major weapon systems. Over the next 40 years, the process for acquiring weapon systems set forth in the 5000 series was revised more than a dozen times—a change approximately once every three years. In some cases, the changes have been dramatic. The 5000 series documents have been issued and reissued, with different versions ranging in length from as few as 8 to as many as 840 pages. These regulatory changes also modified the number of milestones and other decision points required for approval from two, to three, to as many as seven. The documentation required for milestone reviews has ranged from one document in 1971 to dozens of documents in 2008.[119]

---

[118] The Army, Air Force, Navy and Marine Corps, Defense Logistics Agency, and U.S. Special Operations Command each have unique supplements.

[119] Based on discussions with analysts and government officials, CRS review of regulations and documentation, and review of academic working papers that have not yet been published. See J. Ronald Fox, *Defense Acquisition Reform: An Elusive Goal - 1960 to 2010*, Harvard Business School, Working Paper 11-120, p. Appendix B, referenced with permission of the author.

Appendix C. Syllabus for the CRS Seminars *Defense Acquisitions: What Can We Learn From Past Reform Efforts?*

The five-session program examines past reform attempts to identify what has been tried before, what has worked, what has not worked, and lessons that can be drawn from these efforts.

Class	Suggested Reading Prior to Class
Overview of Defense Acquisitions: Overview of syllabus, defense acquisition history, prevalent players in the process, environmental effects and constraints, and measures of success for acquisition reform.	For those new to defense acquisitions, please read *Defense Acquisition Reform 1960-2009 – An Elusive Goal*, pages 1-21; 30-33 (Chapter One).
The Foundation of Modern Acquisition Reform (1970-1986): Discuss findings and recommendations of the Fitzhugh and Packard panels; The Nunn-McCurdy Act.	*Report to The President and the Secretary of Defense on the Department of Defense* (Fitzhugh Report, 1970); pages 1-12 & 17-18 (Executive Summary); pages 79-84; pages 93-96. *A Quest for Excellence* (Packard Report, 1986); pages xi-xiii (Forward); pages 41-71 (Chapter Three). CRS Report R41293, *The Nunn-McCurdy Act: Background, Analysis, and Issues for Congress.*
The 1990s: The Perry Report, Section 800 Panel, and More: Review the findings and recommendations from Secretary Perry and the GAO and consider how their perspectives have changed over time. A look at the Section 800 panel.	Acquisition Reform: A Mandate For Change (Perry Report, 1994) Weapons Acquisition: A Rare Opportunity for Lasting Change (GAO, 1992), pages 35-68. The Origins and Development of the Federal Acquisition Streamlining Act (Hon. Jeff Bingaman, 1994). The QDR In Perspective (US Institute for Peace, 2010); pages 03-03. Defense Acquisition: Charting a Course for Lasting Reform (GAO, 2009).
2000-2011: An Analysis of Key Reports and the Impact of War on Acquisition Reform: Review the findings and recommendations of three recent reports on acquisition reform; discuss the impact of Iraq and Afghanistan on defense acquisitions.	*Army Strong: Equipped, Trained and Ready* (2011), pages vii-xxvi (Executive Summary). *Defense Acquisition Performance Assessment Report* (DAPA, 2006), pages vii; 1-16 (Summary). *Getting to Best: Reforming the Defense Acquisition Enterprise* (2009); pages iii; 1-13 (Executive Summary). General Allan ISAF Counter Insurgency Contracting Guidance. CRS Report R43074, *Department of Defense's Use of Contractors to Support Military Operations: Background, Analysis, and Issues for Congress.*
Recent Initiatives: From Better Buying Power to Congressional Action: Discuss the range of ongoing acquisition system initiatives and assess their impact and potential for long-term improvement.	*Better Buying Power Fact Sheet and Implementation* memo. September 2012 DOD memo on end of year obligations. *Performance of the Defense Acquisition System*, 2013 Annual Report, pages iii-iv; 105-112. *Defense Acquisition Reform 1960-2009*, pages 189-207 (Conclusions).

Bibliography of Readings (in order of assignment)

- J. Ronald Fox, *Defense Acquisition Reform 1960-2009: An Elusive Goal* (Center of Military History, 2011), at http://www.history.army.mil/html/books/051/51-3-1/index.html.

- Department of Defense, *Report to the President and the Secretary of Defense on the Department of Defense by the Blue Ribbon Defense Panel*, July 1, 1970, at http://www.google.com/url?sa=t&rct=j&q=&esrc=s&source=web&cd=1&ved=0CCcQFjAA&url=http%3A%2F%2Fwww.dtic.mil%2Fcgi-bin%2FGetTRDoc%3FAD%3DADA013261&ei=S6sUU6fYIOni0gHG9oDYDg&usg=AFQjCNHXnfsT3jYxSK4t-LzkD38HWtqKYQ&bvm=bv.61965928,d.dmQ.

- President's Blue Ribbon Commission on Defense Management, *A Quest for Excellence, Final Report to the President by the President's Blue Ribbon Commission on Defense Management*, June 30, 1986, at http://usacac.army.mil/cac2/CSI/docs/Gorman/06_Retired/01_Retired_1985_90/07_86_PackardCommission_FinalReport/01_PackardCommission_FinalReport.pdf.

- CRS Report R41293, *The Nunn-McCurdy Act: Background, Analysis, and Issues for Congress*, by Moshe Schwartz.

- U.S. General Accounting Office, *Weapons Acquisitions: A Rare Opportunity for Lasting Change*, GAO/NSIAD-93-15, December 1992, at http://www.gao.gov/products/NSIAD-93-15.

- Honorable Jeff Bingaman, "The Origins and Development of the Federal Acquisition Streamlining Act," *Military Law Review*, vol. 145 (Summer 1994), pp. 149-170, at http://heinonline.org/HOL/Page?handle=hein.journals/milrv145&div=7&collection=journals&set_as_cursor=3&men_tab=srchresults#155.

- Honorable William J. Perry, *Acquisition Reform: A Mandate for Change*, Department of Defense, February 9, 1994, at https://dap.dau.mil/policy/Documents/Policy/Acquistion%20Reform%20a%20Mandate%20for%20Change.pdf.

- U.S. Institute for Peace, *The QDR in Perspective: Meeting America's National Security Needs in the 21st Century*, Final Report of the Quadrennial Defense Review Independent Panel, July 28, 2010, at http://www.usip.org/quadrennial-defense-review-independent-panel-/view-the-report.

- U.S. Government Accountability Office, *Defense Acquisitions: Charting a Course for Lasting Reform*, GAO-09-633T, April 30, 2009, at http://www.gao.gov/new.items/d09663t.pdf.

- U.S. Army, *Army Strong: Equipped, Trained and Ready*, Final Report of the 2010 Army Acquisition Review, January 11, 2011, at http://usarmy.vo.llnwd.net/e2/c/downloads/213465.pdf.

- Department of Defense, *Defense Acquisition Performance Assessment Report*, January 2006, at http://www.defense.gov/pubs/pdfs/DAPA%2012-22%20WEB%20Exec%20Summary.pdf.

- Business Executives for National Security, *Getting to Best: Reforming the Defense Acquisition Enterprise*, A Business Imperative for Change from the Task Force on Defense Acquisition Law and Oversight, July, 2009, at http://www.bens.org/document.doc?id=12.

- CRS Report R43074, *Department of Defense's Use of Contractors to Support Military Operations: Background, Analysis, and Issues for Congress*, by Moshe Schwartz.

- Office of the Under Secretary of Defense Acquisition, Technology and Logistics, *Performance of the Defense Acquisition System*, 2013 Annual Report, June 28, 2013, at http://www.acq.osd.mil/docs/Performance%20of%20the%20Def%20Acq%20System%202013%20-%20FINAL%2028June2013.pdf.

- Under Secretary of Defense Robert Hale and Under Secretary of Defense Frank Kendall, *Department of Defense Management of Unobligated Funds; Obligation Rate Tenets*, Office of the Secretary of Defense, September 10, 2012.

- Under Secretary of Defense Frank Kendall, *Implementation Directive for Better Buying Power 2.0 - Achieving Greater Efficiency and Productivity in Defense Spending*, Department of Defense, April 24, 2013.

- Under Secretary of Defense Frank Kendall, *The New Department of Defense Instruction 5000.02*, Department of Defense, Memorandum for the Acquisition Workforce, December 2, 2013.

Author Contact Information

Moshe Schwartz
Specialist in Defense Acquisition
mschwartz@crs.loc.gov, 7-1463